The Role of Data and Analytics in Smart Manufacturing

Ashoka

Copyright © [2023]

Author: Ashoka

Title: The Role of Data and Analytics in Smart Manufacturing

ISBN:

Contents

Chapter 1
Introduction

Chapter 1

1.1 Introduction

The need for control and automation of manufacturing processes has been advancing rapidly and continuously since the advent of the first CNC machines in the 1970s. [1] Historically, manufacturing has been highly dependent on skilled operators, and the quality of manufactured parts has been highly dependent on individual skills. The reliance on skilled labor started declining with the advent of manufacturing automation, which was driven by the need for mass manufacturing and the standardization of manufactured parts by controlling the variation in the output of the manufacturing process. Automation, generally, can be defined as a "technology concerned with performing a process by means of programmed commands combined with automatic feedback control to ensure proper execution of the instructions. The resulting system is capable of operating without human intervention." [8]. There is hardly an aspect of modern life that has not been affected by automation, which has revolutionized those fields where it has been introduced. The infiltration of automation in all aspects of manufacturing in turn gave rise to the need for manufacturing process control. With automatic control, a device or system is forced to achieve a desired output through intelligent instrumentation in an autonomous manner. [7] The control of manufacturing processes has been made possible by the advancements in machine tools and their controllers. In order to determine whether any process is in control, we compare the reference input signal, to be controlled, to the output signal from the plant after adding the different disturbances and noise originating from sensors and other plant elements. This discrepancy, or error, is used to calculate and enforce the necessary corrective action to bring the signal to the desired position or value. This is the concept of feedback

control. A general feedback control loop is shown in figure 1.1.

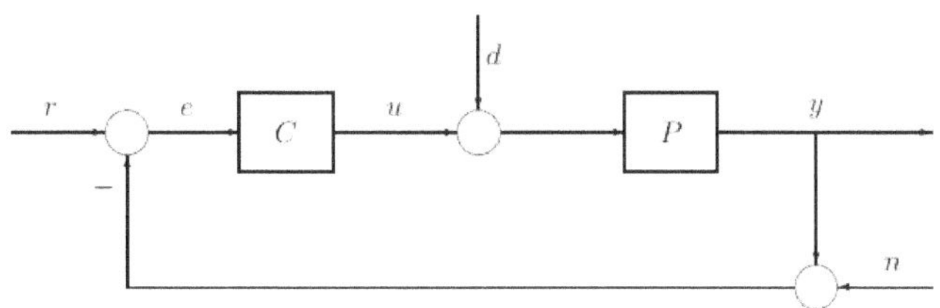

Figure 1: A General Feedback Control Loop

In Figure 1, the boxes labeled P and C represent the Plant and Controller, respectively, while

the other signals displayed on the plot are:

r input signal or reference

e error signal

u Controller output or the control signal

d plant disturbance

y plant output signal

n sensor noise

Historically, the development of the digital computer in the 1940s, along with the

development of integrated circuits, which brought along the advancement in sensors

technology for measuring the different signals in a plant lead to the proliferation and

widespread use of automated feedback control systems. [8] Originally, machinery was

controlled through the use of relays. Relays operate by creating a magnetic force when they

are energized, which pulls a switch into the ON or OFF position. Upon de-energizing the

relay, the switch releases and the device returns to its normal ON/OFF position. [10] Relays

had to be hard-wired in a very precise configuration in order to be able to control the machinery properly. There were a numerous problems and issues with relays as they had to follow a strict maintenance schedule as any issue with any of the relays lead to the failure of the whole system. [10] As a result of these concerns pertaining to the use of relays as well as the important developments in computer processors as well as the availability of and improvements in software to write computer programs, lead to the introduction of the first Programmable Logic Controller (PLC). The PLC is composed of a few basic parts which are the power supply, a central processing unit (CPU), input/output cards and a backplane that the cards are placed on. [11] In addition to the PLC itself, there are two additional key components: the programming device and the human-machine interface (HMI). An HMI provides a means of displaying information and obtaining inputs, modeling the control system as a whole, while the programming device enables the user to view and modify the code on the PLC. [11] Ever since the introduction of the first PLC in 1968, PLCs have infiltrated all industries and all aspects of manufacturing. PLCs usually require programming, based on the given industrial application, so that they can perform their required function. This program is then downloaded onto the memory of the PLC's CPU after which the PLC is instructed to perform the desired functions. PLC functionality has grown over the years, to the point where many PLCs are now quite sophisticated and capable of executing complex, adaptive routines. As semiconductor chips continue to shrink and become more powerful, smaller controllers are becoming more intelligent and more capable aided by the continuous advancements and developments of motion control, vision systems, and communication protocols. [12] Currently, the advancements in data-acquisition systems, information technology, and network technologies has propelled us into the era of 'Industry 4.0'. [13] The term 'Industry 4.0' has been first coined in Germany in 2011 as part of the German government's effort to describe their manufacturing digitization initiative and it has spread all over the world ever since. [14] As a result, smart technologies such as "the Internet of Things (IoT), cloud computing (CC), big data analytics (BDA), cyber–physical systems (CPS), and digital twins (DTs) are taking a central position in new-generation intelligent manufacturing—that is, smart manufacturing." [13] In the United States, The National Institute of Standards and Technology (NIST) and the Department of Energy (DoE) are two organizations that have coined the term "smart manufacturing." [16] Smart manufacturing is defined by Wallace & Riddick [15] as a "data intensive application of information technology at the shop floor level and above to enable intelligent, efficient, and responsive operations." This current focus on 'Industry 4.0' and smart manufacturing and being in the era of big data and the IoT emphasizes the shift in manufacturing from "knowledge-based intelligent manufacturing to data-driven and knowledge-enabled smart manufacturing, in which the term smart refers to the creation and use of data." [13]

Chapter 2:Motivation

Chapter 2

2.1 Motivation

Fiber optic technology has been at the cornerstone of the high-speed data transmission and communication technologies. This technology has been one of the key enablers for the modern age of big data and the IoT. As a result, there has been an explosive growth in the manufacturing of optical fibers driven by the growing needs of our data-driven world. MIT's Device Realization Lab (DRL), in partnership with Sterlite Technologies Ltd. (hereinafter referred to as Sterlite) is developing innovative strategies and approaches to improve the optic fiber manufacturing process, particularly the controller design, simulation, tuning and deployment process. There are many challenges related to the simulation of the inner workings of an industrial process in order for the simulation to be able to capture the different dependencies and intricacies of the system or plant in question. These simulations and models are created using one of three methods below [18]:

1. **White-box models**, where creating a model requires thorough understanding of the underlying physics.
2. **Black-box models**, which are created only using input-output data and don't require an understanding of the internal workings.
3. **Grey-box models**, which combine measurable data with loosely modeled physics and are hybrids of the first two methods.

Moreover, other models need to be generated to simulate the controllers that control and govern the process which are then used to create a complete closed-loop simulation of the entire plant. Traditionally, controller tuning is performed in a trial-and-error manner in a production plant – where a human adjusts a certain parameter, observes the output, then using simple models and intuition to decide which parameter to adjust next, repeat the process until performance is satisfactory. [18] The major drawback of this approach is that it is hugely labor and time intensive. Furthermore, mechanical systems are often constrained by practical safety measures, preventing them from receiving any arbitrary control inputs [18]. System integration may require multiple iterations of design and debugging if multiple controllers need to be developed simultaneously to achieve production quality. As a result of such modifications, production often suffers, and monetary costs rise. [18] This research project focuses on refining and improving the black-box model for the plant and testing the closed-loop simulation for the entire plant along with the controllers to make sure that the model accurately emulates the performance of the fiber extrusion tower. Moreover, this research project focuses on the intersection between modeling and simulation, through Machine Learning (ML), and manufacturing process control and studies how to deploy ML models to industrial controllers such as PLCs. The deployment of ML models on industrial PLCs is a multi-phase process and the different phases of the deployment process are below:

1. **Phase 1**: Use the optimized one-time gain settings retuned by the ML model with existing controllers to optimize the process

2. **Phase 2**: Slow evolution of optimized gains, where the gains are changed manually as changes in the production system occur

3. **Phase 3**: Utilizing new hard-ware along with the ML model to automate the gain settings changes

4. **Phase 4**: Using the new hardware with new model architecture and new algorithms beyond Proportional-Integral-Derivative (PID) control.

A method for providing a proof-of-concept for the use of ML models to produce gains that can be used for optimizing the fiber extrusion process will be highlighted using an industrial PLC and a desktop **Fiber Extrusion Device** (FrED) [18] that was developed by the DRL at the Massachusetts Institute of Technology (MIT). Finally, conclusions on current work recommendations for future work will be provided.

2.2 Optical Fiber Extrusion Process

The high-level optical fiber manufacturing process is depicted below in Figure 2.

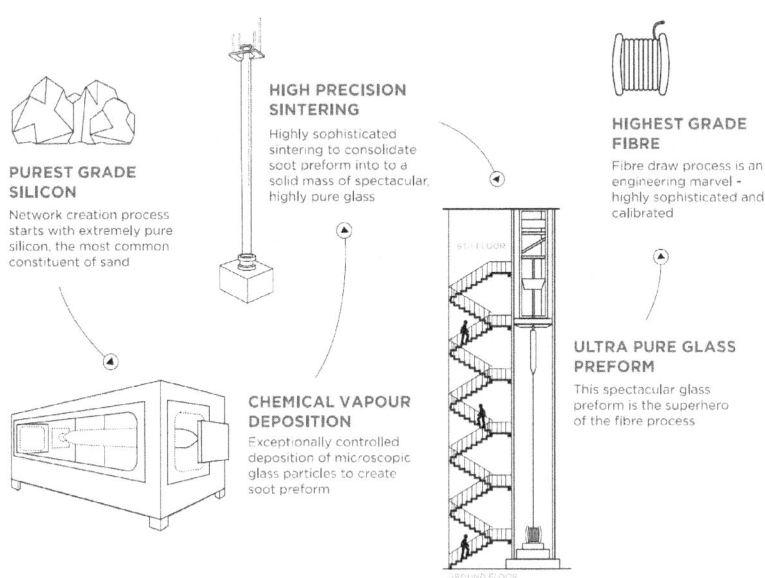

Figure 2: High Level Optic Fiber Manufacturing Process[17]

The basis for the optical fiber is high grade silica which then goes through soot deposition, which is the most important process in optic fiber manufacturing process as it plays a very significant role in determining the optical properties of the produced fiber. Soot deposition is a form of Open Vapor Deposition where Silicon Chloride ($SiCl_4$) vapor, doped with

Germania, is transported through a carrier medium to burners where they are then deposited on mandrels. The mandrel with the deposited soot then gets transported to a sintering machine where it is heated to a temperature below the melting point which results in the particles diffusing into a solid glass piece. The sintered glass is then immediately sent to a soaking furnace where it is soaked at high temperatures to release any entrapped gases and to relieve any thermal stress on the glass. The previous processes result in a mother preform which then goes through a draw tower to be drawn into smaller rods. The mother preform goes through an induction furnace where the preform is drawn at the softening temperature of the glass into smaller core rods. These core rods are the then tested to determine whether their optical properties are within the required range and if they pass the quality inspection, they go through to the cladding phase. The cladding phase is where the addition of new layers of soot are added to the core rod for it reach its final diameter The cylindrical rod preforms are then slowly and continuously fed through a draw furnace while keeping the appropriate tension to control the diameter of the produced optical fiber. During the fiber extrusion process, the preform experiences a drastic change in its diameter where it goes from a few centimeters in diameter preform to the micron-level fiber. An industrial fiber extrusion tower on the shop floor is shown in Figure 3.

Figure 3: A Fiber Extrusion Production Tower

As the fiber leaves the furnace, it is then cooled in a dedicated cooling unit with Helium injection before being spooled onto a capstan, that maintains the drawing force. Finally, a double layer of fiber coating is cured onto the fiber surface using ultraviolet curing to produce optical fibers. A simplified illustration of the fiber extrusion tower with its components is shown in Figure 4. Multiple sensors and controllers work to measure the real-time parameters of the fiber draw process for the controllers to be manipulated.

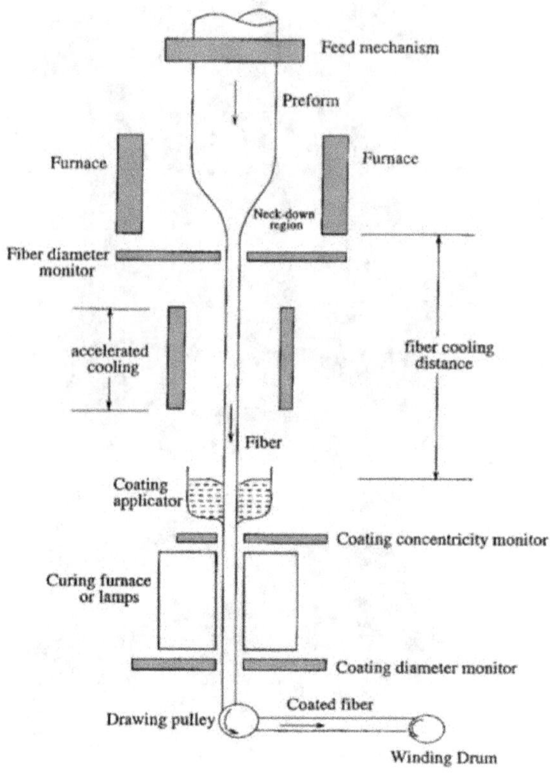

Figure 4: Simplified Illustration of a Fiber Draw Tower with its Components

The main inputs of the draw tower that control the diameter of the produced fiber (Bare Fiber Diameter (BFD)) are the furnace power, the speed at which the preform goes into the furnace, the capstan speed, on which the fiber is spooled, and the helium temperature, that is used to cool the produced fiber. The outputs of the system that are used for feedback control are the diameter of the fiber and the tension. There are three controllers that control the signals that manage and regulate the fiber extrusion process and are highlighted in red boxes in Figure 5.

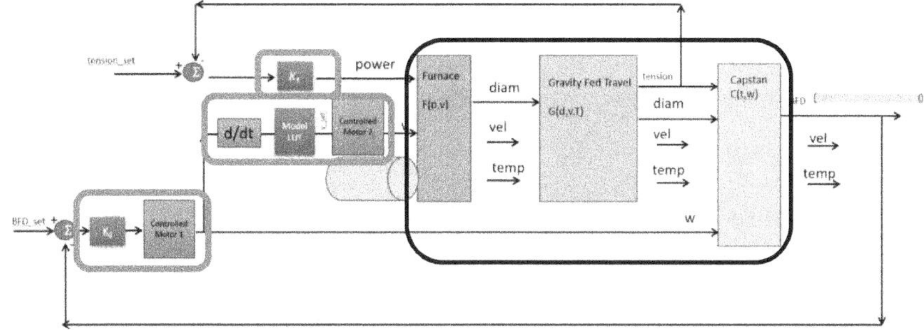

Figure 5: A schematic of the optical fiber drawing system provided by Sterlite.

The three controllers that govern the fiber extrusion process are the tension controller, K_t, which is a PID controller that takes as its input the error in the measured tension and outputs a corrective signal to the radiation furnace. The diameter controller, labeled as K_d, is also a PID controller that takes error in the measured BFD as its input and outputs a corrective signal to the capstan to control its velocity accordingly. Finally, the preform velocity controller, the middle box in Figure 5, involves a discrete look-up table that correlates the acceleration of the capstan, the slope of the capstan speed, to the preform speed. The output signals of the system that are used for feedback control are the tension and the BFD. [19]

2.3 Previous Work

There is an abundant amount of work and research done on the fiber extrusion process that detail the physics of the system and how it is affected by the different inputs. Moreover, the field of industrial controls is widely understood. However, there has not yet been a full exploration of the data-driven approach to controller design in the manufacturing field. Furthermore, this research project will make use of the desktop Fiber Extrusion Device

(FrED) that was developed by David Donghyun Kim as part of his doctoral research at MIT's Device Realization Lab. FrED was developed as an educational tool to teach students and professional about feedback control systems and manufacturing and it could be used as a prototyping tool to "explore new designs or fabricate new types of fiber." [20] Moreover, George Chen and Victor Reyes, as part of their master's book at MIT's DRL, came up with a MATLAB™ code to simulate the fiber drawing tower for Sterlite. Chen and Reyes built a Long Short-Term Memory (LSTM) Neural Network model for the aggregate plant as well as different models for the different controllers in an attempt to construct a closed-loop simulation for the entire plant.

2.4 Book Overview

This book builds upon and utilizes the previous work highlighted above. The previous model created by Chen and Reyes will be highlighted, modified, and improved upon to create a more general model for the optical fiber draw tower. Multiple iterations of the black-box model of the system were designed using different neural networks architectures and configurations to determine their input-output relationships. Moreover, the process for controlling FrED using an industrial PLC is highlighted along with the feedback loop to control the diameter of the fiber. Also, recommendations for next steps to complete the different phases of this ongoing project are provided. Chapter 3 of this book gives a theoretical background of machine learning in general and LSTMs in particular. Chapter 4 describes the modifications and improvements made on the model and highlights the new results obtained using the new trained model with the new configuration. Chapter 5 highlights the process of connecting FrED to the PLC along with the hardware used for controlling FrED through the PLC and provides the feedback control loop used to control the diameter of the fiber. Finally, Chapter

6 gives the conclusions of this work and recommendations for future work.

Chapter 3:Machine Learning as a modeling tool

Chapter 3

3.1 Machine Learning as a modeling tool

Fundamentally, the focus of Machine Learning (ML) is "making decisions or predictions based on data." [21] There are several classes of problems that can be solved using machine learning. These classes vary based on the kind of data that is provided and what conclusions are to be drawn from them. Some of the broad classes of Machine Learning are highlighted below:

1. **Supervised learning,** where the inputs and the outputs of the system are known. Supervised learning is divided into regression or classification based on the dataset and the conclusions to be drawn from the data

2. **Unsupervised learning,** where we are not interested in finding a correlation or a function between a set of input-output pairs, but rather we are interested in finding some patterns or structure inherent in the data

3. **Reinforcement learning,** where we are trying to learn a mapping from inputs to outputs without specifying which inputs are best to maximize the desired output. In reinforcement learning, the ML model interacts with the environment to learn to maximize its reward

4. **Sequence learning,** where the aim is to learn an output sequence from an input sequence where the sequences are depicted as states of the model [21]

5. **Transfer learning,** where the goal is to use experience from previous tasks and apply to "learning a current task in a way that requires decreased experience with the new task." [21]

Machine Learning has garnered significant interest of late and has been at the forefront of everyday life as it has penetrated every aspect of life, from Netflix's recommendations system to self-driving cars. [2] According to a recent study conducted by Deloitte, 67% of companies in the top 11 economies are using machine learning, and 97% percent are planning to use it within a year. [2] This has been made possible by technological advances in data processing and cloud storge, that has made tremendous amounts of data available at the click of a button. The field of Machine Learning was motivated by the hope of creating a machine that functions and processes information like the human brain. Early research into Machine Learning dates to the 1940s, which was when the first definition of Machine Learning was coined by Arthur Samuel in 1950 as "the field of study that gives computers the ability to learn without explicitly being programmed." [3] Artificial Neural Networks (ANNs) are a sub-field of Machine Learning, which owes its existence to the work of McCulloch and Pitts in 1943, who created the first computational model of a neuron. [4] ANNs mimic the way a neuron functions in the human brain. A neuron is a cell in the human brain that is responsible for receiving inputs from the outside world, sending signals to muscles, and relaying the electrical signals at every step in between. [5] The neuron can be divided into three parts namely, dendrites, cell body, and axon. The dendrite is responsible for receiving signals from other neurons. The cell body is responsible for processing all the information that comes from the dendrites, and then outputs that information to neighboring neurons through the axons. [6] Similarly, the artificial neuron, which is the building block of ANNs, consists of three main parts. The inputs (dendrites) get passed through to an activation function, that acts as the cell body, which then gives an output, analogous to the function of the axon as seen in Figure 6.

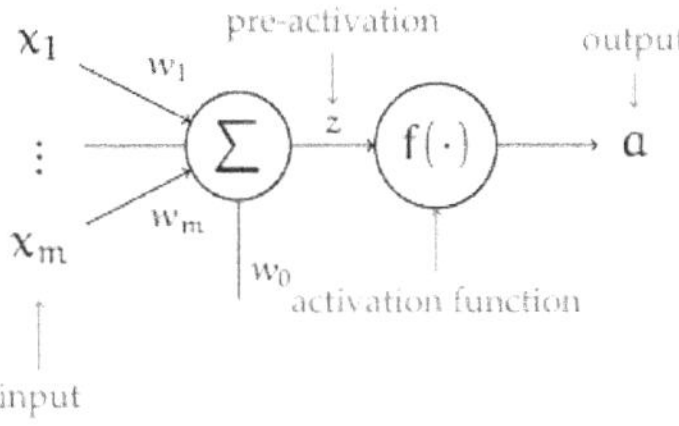

Figure 6: Layout of an Artificial Neuron [21]

3.2 Neural Networks Definitions and Nomenclature

The basic element of a neural network is the 'neuron' depicted above in Figure 6. The neuron can be thought of as a non-linear function of the input vector $\mathbf{x} \in \mathbb{R}^m$, where m is the number of inputs, to a single output value $y \in \mathbb{R}$. The neuron is parametrized by a vector of weights $(w_1, \ldots, w_m) \in \mathbb{R}^m$ and a scalar offset $w_0 \in \mathbb{R}$. The activation function represented by the neuron can be expressed as

$$y = f(z) = f\left(\left(\sum_{j=1}^{m} x_j w_j\right) + w_0\right) = f(w^T x + w_0) \tag{3.1}$$

where z is the pre-activation function

$$z = w^T x + w_0 \tag{3.2}$$

A neural network is a combination of multiple neurons that create a network. Most neural networks are feed-forward neural networks as data flows only one way from the inputs to the output and the function computed by the network is a "composition of the functions computed by the individual neurons." [21] An illustration of a feed-forward neural network is provided in Figure 7 where the first layer is called the input layer, the last layer is the output layer, and all intermediate layers are called hidden layers and they can be interpreted as "intermediate or internal representations of the information." [19]

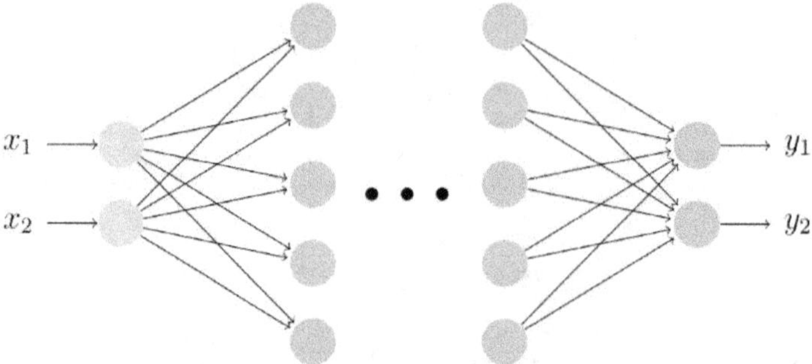

Figure 7: Illustration of a feed-forward neural network. The input, hidden and output layers are shown in blue, grey, and green, respectively [19]

Given that each neuron has a vector or weights and an offset, the weights of the whole layer could be grouped together into a matrix W, and all the offsets could be grouped into W_0, resulting in an output vector of

$$Y = f(W^T x + W_0) \tag{3.2}$$

There are numerous choices of activation functions that are chosen based on the application and the conclusions that are to be drawn from the data. Table 1 provides a list of the most common activation functions used in machine learning today.

3.3 Evaluating Neural Networks

Once the problem class has been specified and the appropriate activation function has been chosen, we need criteria that enables us to determine how good the prediction made by the trained model is. The quality of the prediction of a machine learning model is expressed in terms of a loss function J. Table 2 specifies some of the different loss functions used with different applications of machine learning, where g is the guess predicted by the model and a is the actual value that we are trying to predict.

Activation Function	Graph	Usage
Step function $$\text{step}(z) = \begin{cases} 0 & z < 0 \\ 1 & z \geq 0 \end{cases}$$	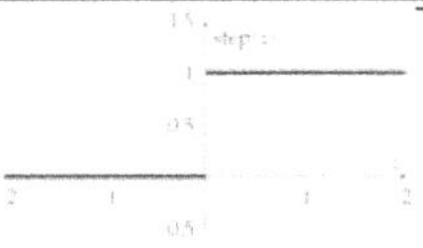	Binary (0-1) loss
Linear Function $$f(z) = z$$	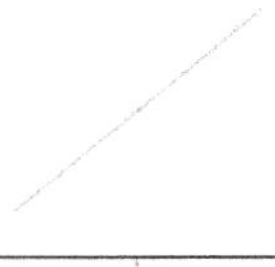	Passthrough
Sigmoid/Logistic function $$\sigma(z) = \frac{1}{1 + e^{-z}}$$	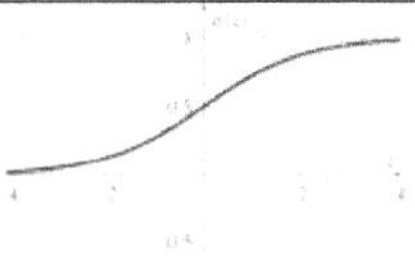	Regression
Hyperbolic Tangent (tanh) $$\tanh(z) = \frac{e^z - e^{-z}}{e^z + e^{-z}}$$	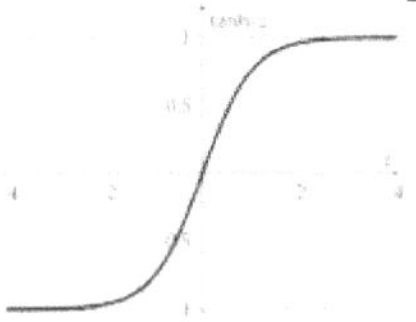	Normalizing data
Softmax function $$\text{softmax}(\mathbf{z}) = \frac{\exp(\mathbf{z})}{\sum_j \exp(z_j)}$$	N/A	Multi-class classification
Rectified Linear Unit (ReLU) $$\text{ReLU}(z) = \begin{cases} 0 & z < 0 \\ z & z \geq 0 \end{cases} = \max(0, z)$$	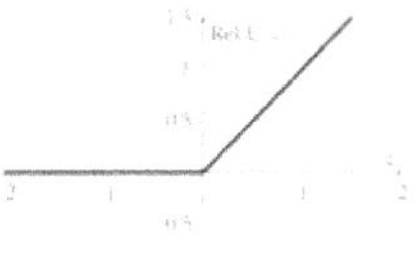	CNNs
Leaky ReLU $$\text{LReLU}(z) = \begin{cases} \alpha z & z < 0 \\ z & z \geq 0 \end{cases}, \alpha > 0$$	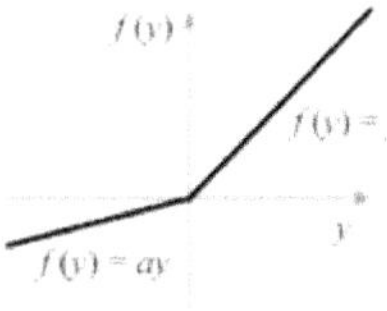	CNNs

Table 1: Most common activation functions in Machine Learning with their functions, graphs, and usage [19]

Name	Equation	Usage
0-1 Loss	$\mathcal{L}(g, a) = \begin{cases} 0 & \text{if } g = a \\ 1 & \text{otherwise} \end{cases}$	Predictions drawn from finite domains
Linear Loss	$L(g, a) = \lvert g - a \rvert$	Regression
Squared Loss	$L(g, a) = (g - a)^2$	Preferred method for regression
Cross-entropy Loss	$L(g, a) = -[g \, log(a) + (1 - a) \, log(1 - g)]$	Classification

Machine learning problems can be thought of as optimization problems where we are trying to learn the weights w of the model that minimize the loss function, otherwise known as the objective function or the cost function. The objective function for a regression problem, using squared loss can be written as

$$J(w, w_0) = \frac{1}{n} \sum_{i=1}^{n} \left(w^T x^{(i)} + w_0 - y^{(i)} \right)^2 \tag{3.4}$$

The goal of the machine learning algorithm is to learn the weights w and w_0 that minimize equation 3.4. This is performed through variants of gradient descent approaches. [19] Gradient descent is the process of finding the lowest point on the surface that defines $J(w)$. The weights are gradually updated, according to Equation 3.5, by taking the gradient of the objective function with respect to the corresponding weight, in the direction opposite to the gradient. The size of the step, known in the literature as the learning rate, that we take in the direction opposite to the gradient is an important hyperparameter that needs to be selected carefully as it controls whether we converge towards the optimal solution or diverge away from it.

$$w_{new} = w_{old} - \eta \left(\frac{dJ}{dw_{old}} \right) \qquad (3.5)$$

A very high learning rate would cause the solution to converge and not reach the minimum while a low learning rate will take a long time to reach the minimum which is not computationally efficient. Figure 8 shows the effect of the learning rate on reaching the optimum solution, where we initialize the weights at the point marked with the blue x. The left side of Figure 8 with a high step size of 0.3 cause divergence away from the optimum solution while the step size of 0.04 cause the solution to converge to the minimum.

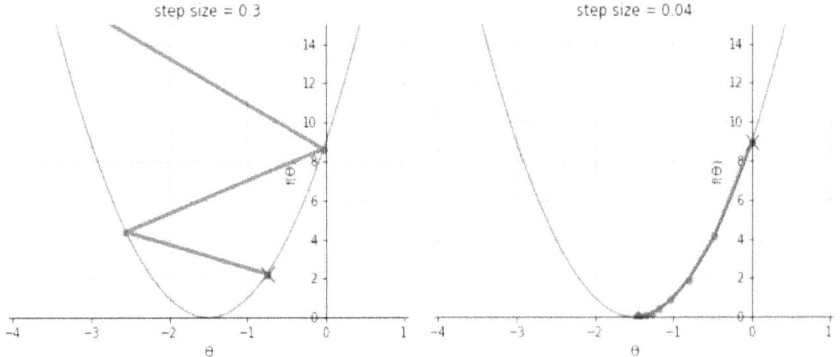

Figure 8: Effect of Learning Rate on Loss Minimization

Deep learning refers to the process of developing large neural network models that can make accurate decisions based on data. [22] Deep learning networks are neural networks that have at least two hidden layers between the input and output layers. An advantage of deep learning is that it is suitable for contexts with large datasets and complex data, such as speech recognition, natural language processing and time-series data. The training process for deep neural networks involves dividing the large dataset into multiple batches and iterating over the dataset for multiple epochs. [19] During an epoch, a batch of data is trained by the network and the weights of the different neurons in the network are obtained based on the loss function specified. The quality of the training is affected by different hyperparameters such as the learning rate, the batch size, and the number of epochs. One subset of deep learning and deep neural networks is Recurrent Neural Networks (RNNs) which are particularly useful for analyzing time-series data and which are used to train the models for this project.

3.4 Recurrent Neural Networks

Recurrent Neural Networks (RNNs) were developed and tailored to the processing of sequential data. [22] RNNs differ from the conventional feed-forward neural networks in that they have a memory buffer where they store the output of the hidden layer and "feeds it back into the hidden layer along with the next input from the sequence." [22] RNNs are modeled after state machines whose basic diagram is depicted below in Figure 9 and whose equations are shown in Equations 3.6 and 3.7, where the current state s_t is defined by the transition function, $f_s(.)$, which takes an input and a previous state and produces the current state. The output, y_t, is defined by the output function, f_o, which takes as its input the current state and produces an output.

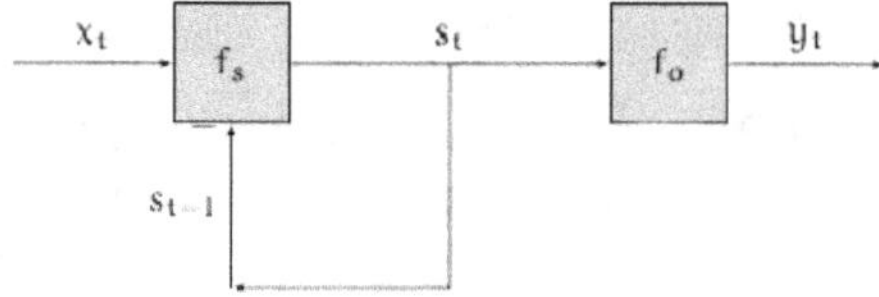

Figure 9: Illustration of a State Machine [21]

$$s_t = f_s(s_{t-1}, x_t) \tag{3.6}$$

$$y_t = f_o(s_t) \tag{3.7}$$

In matrix notation, Equations 3.6 and 3.7 can be expressed as

$$s_t = f_s(W^{sx}x_t + W^{ss}s_{t-1} + W_0{}^{ss}) \tag{3.8}$$

$$y_t = f_o(W^o s_t + W_0{}^o) \tag{3.9}$$

The loss function used to train RNNs is the summation of all the per-element losses on each of the output values as shown in Equation 3.10, where L_{seq} is the loss over the entire sequence and L_{elt} is the per-element loss.

$$L_{seq}\left(g^{(i)}, y^{(i)}\right) = \sum_{t=1}^{n^{(i)}} L_{elt}\left(g^{(i)}, y^{(i)}\right) \tag{3.10}$$

The goal is then to minimize the objective function

$$J(W) = \frac{1}{q}\sum_{i=1}^{q} L_{seq}\left(RNN\left(x^{(i)}; W\right), y^{(i)}\right) \tag{3.11}$$

The weights of the matrices in the Equation 3.11 are trained using Back-Propagation Through Time (BPTT). BPTT is the process of unrolling the RNN to model the sequence so that it can be treated as a feed-forward neural network which facilitates finding the network gradients that enable the minimization of the objective function. Figure 10 shows an example of an unrolled RNN with 3 inputs.

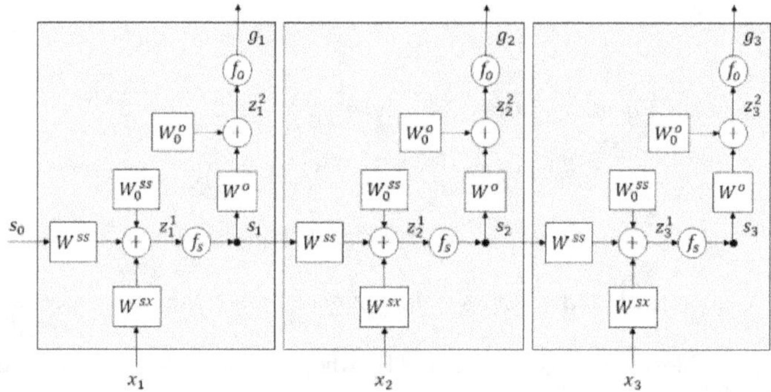

Figure 10: Example of an Unrolled RNN with 3 Inputs

One feature of RNNs and BPTT is that the gradient is shared among the different layers. Generally, this results in the weights shrinking or growing exponentially with the length of the sequence, which poses a problem while training the network due to the error propagating backward throughout the entire sequence. [21][22] This phenomenon is known as vanishing gradients or exploding gradients, respectively. As a result of this drawback with RNNs, Long Short-Term Memory Networks (LSTMs) were developed as they tackle this issue. LSTMs are used in this research project to train the sequences of inputs for the optical fiber draw tower and predict the required outputs and are explained in the following section.

3.5 Long Short-Term Memory Networks

Long Short-Term Memory Networks (LSTMs) are a subset of RNNs have recently emerged as the network of choice for several learning problems dealing with temporal and sequential data as they are especially effective in "capturing long-term temporal dependencies." [23] The LSTM architecture is based on the core concept of a "memory cell, which can maintain its state over time, and non-linear gating units, which regulate the information flow into and out of the cell." [23] The memory cell is where the vector of activations is stored and propagated forwards while being controlled by three non-linear gates. These gates are

1. **The forget gate,** which determines which inputs should be forgotten at which time step using a sigmoid activation function

2. **The input gate,** which determines how the cell activations should be updated in response to the new input. The input gate uses a combination of sigmoid and Tanh activation functions.

3. **The output gate,** which generates the output of the network in response to the current input. [22]

An illustration of the internal structure of an LSTM is shown in Figure 11.

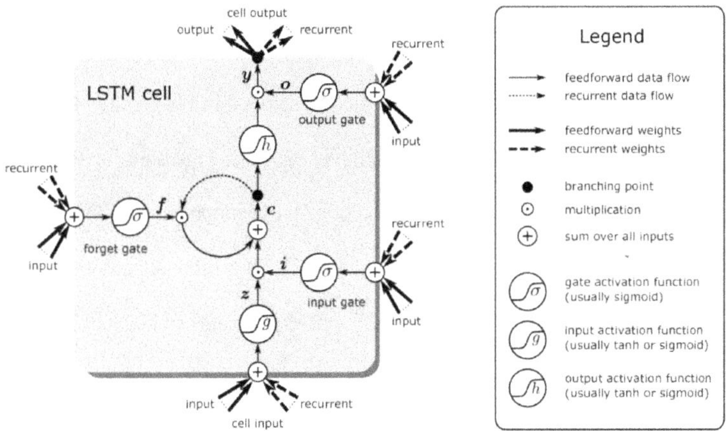

Figure 11: Internal Architecture of an LSTM [24]

The set of equations below govern the operations that happen inside an LSTM [24];

$$z_t \; = \; g(W_z x_t \; + \; U_z y_{t-1} \; + \; b_z) - \; Cell\; Input \tag{3.12}$$

$$i_t \; = \; \sigma(W_i x_t \; + \; U_i y_{t-1} \; + \; b_i) - \; Input\; Gate \tag{3.13}$$

$$f_t \; = \; \sigma\big(W_f x_t \; + \; U_f y_{t-1} \; + \; b_f\big) - \; Forget\; Gate \tag{3.14}$$

$$c_t \; = \; i_t.z_t \; + \; f_t.c_{t-1} - \; Cell\; State \tag{3.15}$$

$$o_t = \sigma(W_o x_t + U_o y_{t-1} + b_o) - Output\ Gate \tag{3.16}$$

$$y_t = o_t.h(c_t) - Cell\ Output \tag{3.17}$$

where $\sigma(.)$ is the sigmoid activation function and $g(.)$ and $h(.)$ are the tanh activation functions. The above architecture and governing equations are for the most basic LSTM architecture, dubbed *Vanilla LSTM.* [23] There are various variants on the Vanilla LSTM architecture explored in the literature, some of which are the Bi-Directional LSTM, which examines both past and future information to produce the cell output. [19] Other variants explored different arrays of LSTM networks stacked either horizontally or vertically. [19] These variants will be explored further in Section 4.2.2, as they will be compared and used to determine the best architecture for the black box model of the optical fiber drawing tower. The experimental setup for the research project is detailed in Chapter 4 which is divided into two main parts. The first part details the setup of the Fiber Extrusion Device (FrED) with an industrial PLC to be used as proof of concept of the deployment of a ML model to control the diameter of the extruded fiber using a PLC. The second part explores the model optimization for the draw tower and the different experiments conducted.

Chapter 4: Experimental Setup

Chapter 4: Experimental Setup

4.1 Connecting PLC to Desktop Fiber Extrusion Device

4.1.1 Fiber Extrusion Device (FrED)

The desktop Fiber Extrusion Device (FrED) was developed by David Donghyun Kim as part of his doctoral research at the Device Realization Lab at MIT. [18] FrED was developed and introduced to model the optical fiber manufacturing process for education purposes to teach smart manufacturing. [20] The first FrED that was developed is shown in Figure 12. Since the development of the first FrED, several modifications and improvements were made to the system. Shirley Lu, as part of her master research at MIT, developed an accumulator for the fiber that is produced by FrED to allow for longer periods of fiber production by FrED to acquire more data that can be used in the aforementioned educational setting. [25] More recently, Shreya Dhar developed a modified FrED that measures the tension on the produced fiber as well as its diameter.

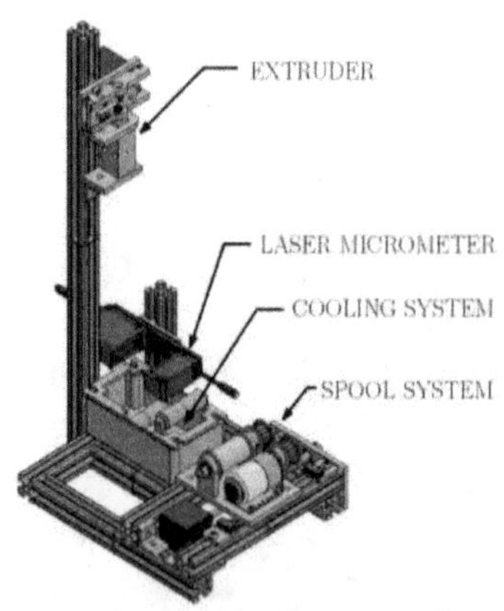

Figure 12: Desktop Fiber Extrusion Device for Education [18]

Analogous to the optical fiber production tower, a preform (glue stick) is heated up using a heating element, shown in Figure 13, and then the preform is pushed through the heating element with the help of a stepper motor. The heated fiber than goes through a cooling system and is then collected on a spool that is a run by a DC motor. The DC motor is housed on a carriage that moves axially to distribute the collected fiber over the entire spool and the boundaries of the movement of the carriage are controlled by limit switches. The diameter of the produced fiber is measured through a laser micrometer and is used as the input signal for the closed feedback control loop.

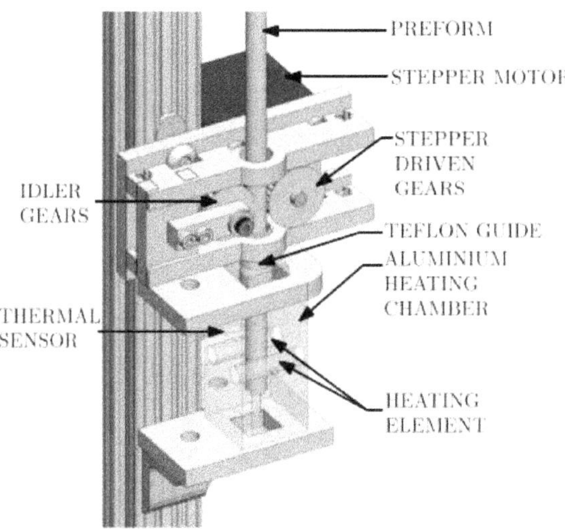

Figure 13: Extrusion System of Fred [18]

FrED employed several sensors to measure the different parameters and to create the feedback loop that controls the diameter of the system. The feedback loop developed by Kim [18] is shown in Figure 14, where the output of the Proportional-Integral (PI) controller, that is used to control the rotational velocity of the spool motor, is based on the error of the measured diameter to the target diameter of the fiber. Moreover, the system was controlled using an Arduino script modeling a simple closed-loop controller.

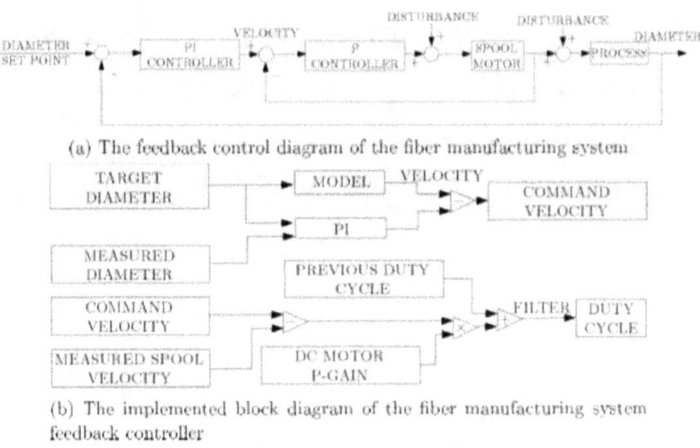

Figure 14: Fiber Extrusion Device Feedback Controller [18]

As part of the ongoing project with Sterlite to deploy the ML model developed for their optical fiber drawing tower onto an industrial PLC to automatically control their extrusion process and maintain a consistent fiber diameter, FrED is used as a proof-of-concept of the deployment process. The next section details the process of connecting the different components and element of FrED to the PLC.

4.1.2 Controlling FrED through PLC

Allen-Bradley's CompactLogix 5380 industrial PLC was used to control FrED throughout this research project. The CompactLogix 5380 is shown below in Figure 15.

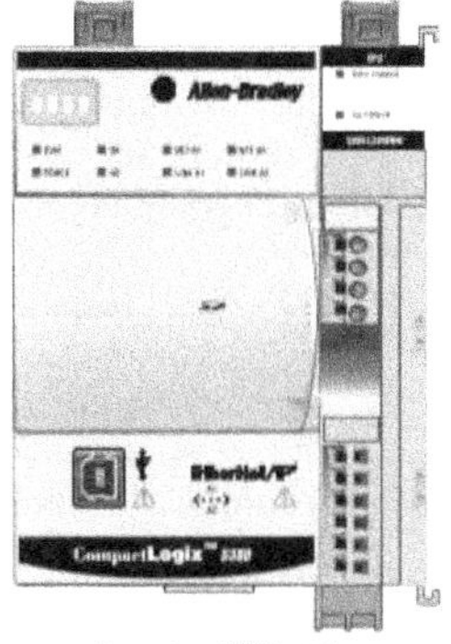

CompactLogix 5380 Controller

Figure 15: Allen-Bradley's CompactLogix 5380 PLC [26]

This PLC is a standalone controller that comes with a chassis on which other modules can be connected to the PLC through the backplane or through more complex systems with devices connected to it through an EtherNet network. The PLC is controlled and managed through Studio 5000™ proprietary software and is connected to a laptop or desktop through an EtherNet connection at the bottom of the PLC as shown in Figure 16.

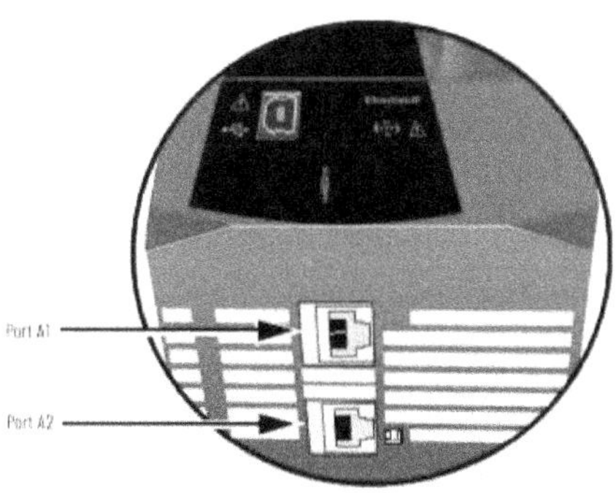

Figure 16: EtherNet Connection at the bottom of PLC [26]

The CompactLogix 5380 PLC used has 4 modules connected to it, namely, the DC Input module, 5069-IB16F, the DC Output module, 5069-OB16F, a counter module and an Analog Input module, 5069-IY4, whose wiring diagrams are found in Appendix A. Both the DC Input and DC output modules are 10…32V DC 16-point modules, meaning that they can accommodate up to 16 different channels, based on the application. There are several components of FrED, discussed in Section 4.1.1, that need to be connected to the PLC so that it can be controlled. Those are two NEMA-17 Stepper Motors, A DC Motor, the heater RTD, the Keyence IG-028 laser micrometer sensor head unit paired with the IG-1000 amplifier unit and the two limit switches.

4.1.2.1 Connecting Stepper Motors to PLC

FrED has two stepper motors that govern the motion of the preform (glue stick) and the carriage on which the spool DC motor is housed. In order to control the stepper motors through the PLC, a stepper driver is needed to interface between the PLC's step and direction signals and the stepper motor. For this purpose, two Advanced Motion Controls Inc. (AMCI) SD4840E2 Networked Stepper Indexers/Drivers were used to control the two stepper motors. The stepper driver receives power from an external power source to the +Vdc: Main and GND ports shown in Figure 17 below. In order for the PLC to communicate with the driver, an EtherNet cable is connected from the PLC to the one of the drivers and another cable is daisy-chained to the other one. The AMCI SD4840E2 Driver bottom view is shown in Figure 18. Add-On Instructions, such as Move and Jog, were used to control the motion of the stepper motors. The connections between the stepper motors and the drivers are shown in Figure 19 below.

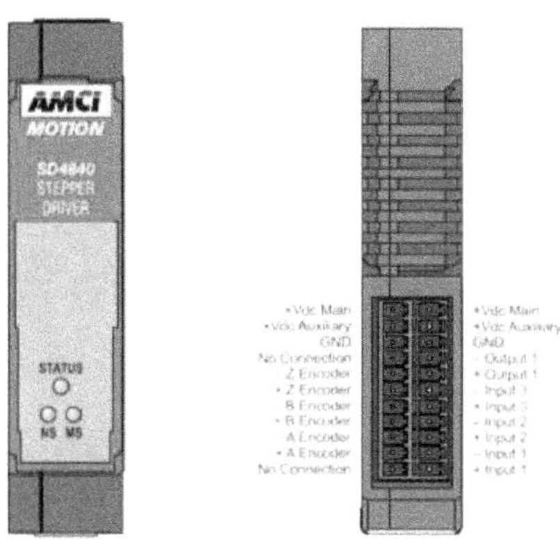

Figure 17: AMCI Stepper Driver Front and Back Panels [27]

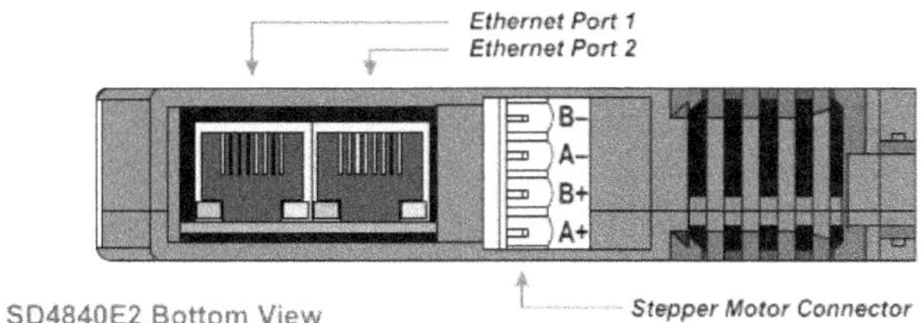

Figure 18: AMCI Stepper Driver Bottom View [27]

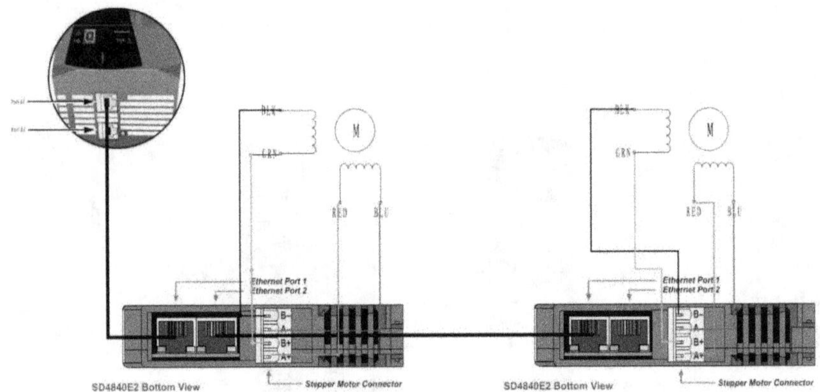

Figure 19: Stepper Motors to AMCI Drivers Connection

4.1.2.2 Connecting Heating Elements to PLC

The heater used to heat the preform (glue stick) to create the neck-down profile to produce the fiber uses two internal heating elements. In order to connect the two heating elements to the PLC, two LGDehome 5V – 36V Dual High Power Drive Boards were used. The two boards were powered by an external power supply and their output was connected to the respective heating elements. The board used is shown below in Figure 20.

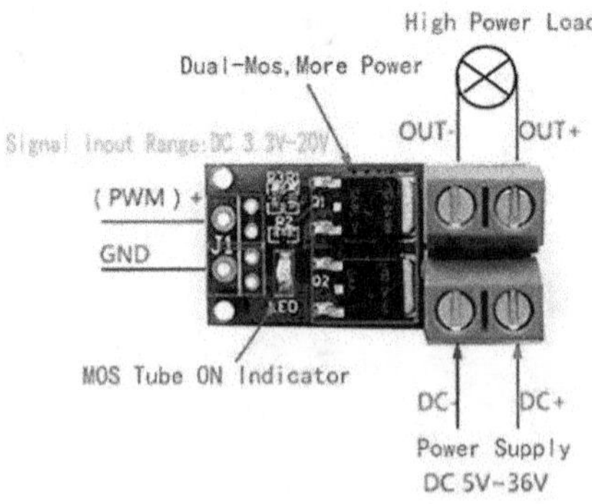

Figure 20: LGDehome High Power Drive Board

The Pulse Width Modulation (PWM) Signal going to the board by which a signal is sent to the heating element and the glue stick is heated is controlled by the DC output module of the PLC. The electrical drawing for the connection between the heating elements, the drive boards, and the PLC as well as the Studio 5000 program that is used to control the heating elements are shown below in Figure 21 and Figure 22, respectively.

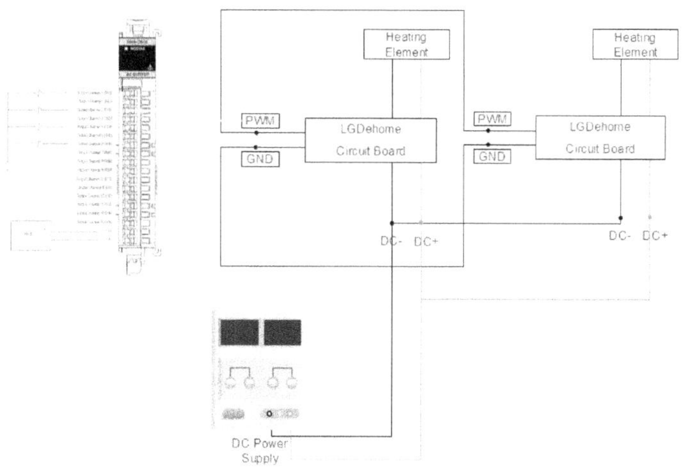

Figure 21: Electrical Drawing for Connection between Heating Elements and PLC

Figure 22: Studio 5000 Program to Control Heating Elements

Moreover, the temperature sensor from the heating element is connected to the Analog Input module on the PLC, in order to be able to record and measure the temperature of the heater, as shown in the Figure 23 below.

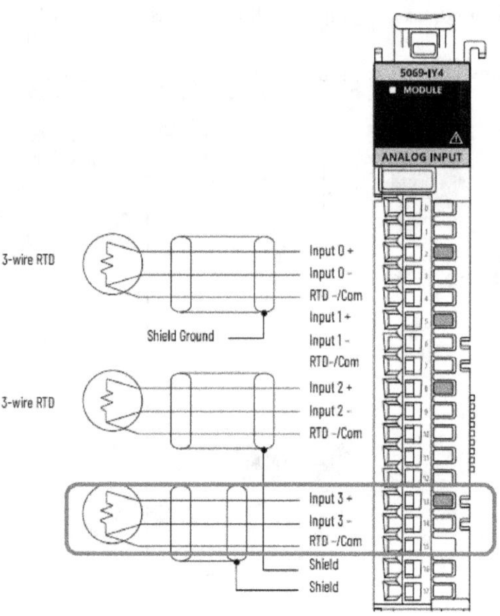

Figure 23: Heating Element Input to Analog Input Module on PLC. The red box highlights where the connection is made to the module

4.1.2.3 Connecting DC Motor to PLC

The DC motor, a Polulu 37D Meatal Gearmotor, is connected to the PLC using the same LGDehome board, shown above in Figure 19, so that it could be controlled through the PLC using PWM signals. The 37D Gearmotor comes with an encoder, which is not needed for the connection between the motor and the PLC. The LGDehome board receives power for the external power supply and its output is connected to the DC motor with the PWM signal coming for the DC output module of the PLC. The electrical drawing for the connection between the different elements and the Studio 5000 program used to control the DC motor are shown below in Figure 24 and Figure 25, respectively. The DC motor is controlled through a Split Range Time Proportional (SRTP) function block that takes the 0-100% output of a PID loop and drives the output contacts with a periodic signal.

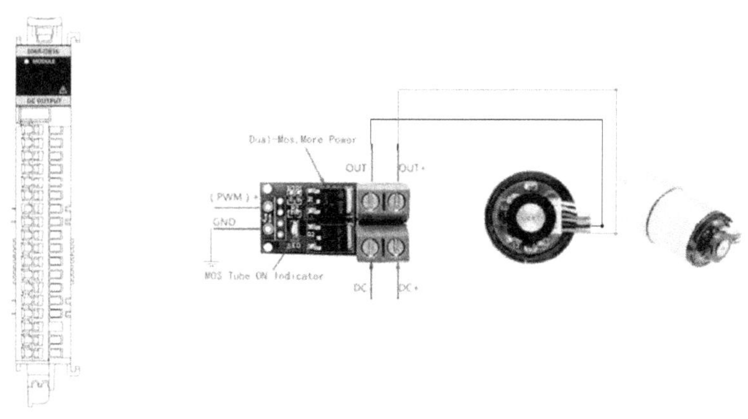

Figure 24: Electrical Schematic of DC Motor Connection to PLC

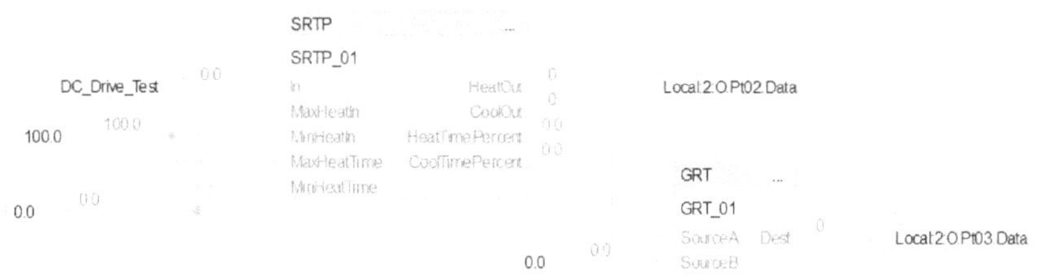

Figure 25: Studio 5000 Program to Control DC Motor

4.1.2.4 Connecting Keyence Laser Micrometer to PLC

The Keyence IG-028 laser micrometer sensor head unit paired with the IG-1000 amplifier unit are connected to the Analog Input module on the PLC. The wiring for the laser micrometer is shown below in Figure 26. The Brown and Blue wires which are power to the sensor are connected to the external power supply and the Light blue wire, that has the Analog output + and the Analog output GND, is connected to the Analog Input module of the PLC.

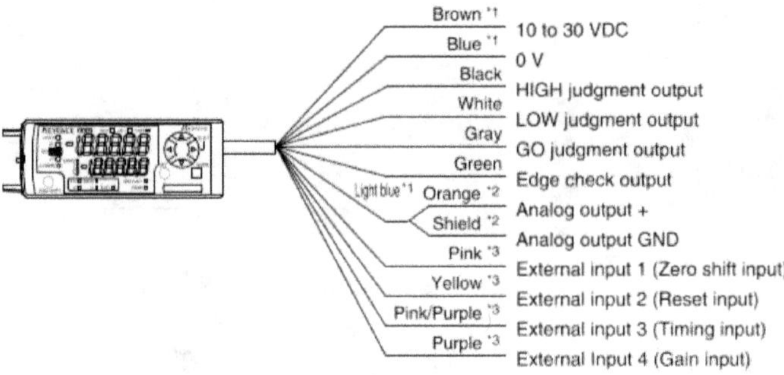

Figure 26: Keyence Laser Micrometer Wiring Schematic

4.1.2.5 Connecting Limit Switches to PLC

The two limit switches on FrED control the translational motion of the carriage that carries the spool. The circuit diagram of a basic limit switch is shown in Figure 27. Power from the external power supply is connected to one terminal of the limit switch, while the other terminal is connected to the DC input module of the PLC, as shown in Figure 28. The above process is repeated for the other limit switch.

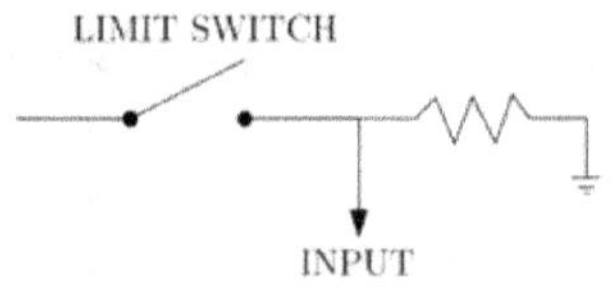

Figure 27: Limit Switch Circuit Diagram [18]

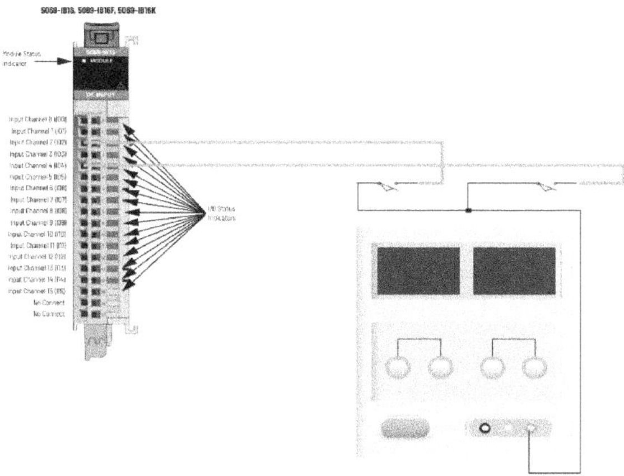

Figure 28: Limit Switches Connection to PLC

When the carriage reaches the end of its motion and hits the limit switch, the limit switch closes, which sends a voltage signal to the PLC. The PLC, consequently, sends a signal to the stepper motor driver to reverse the direction of motion of the motor so that the fiber can be collected over the entire length of the spool.

The PLC with all the connections is shown below in Figure 29.

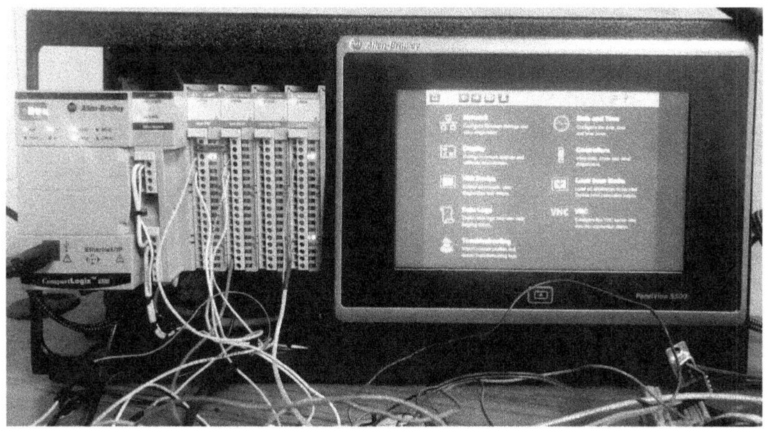

Figure 29: PLC with All Connections

4.2 Optical Fiber Draw Tower Modeling

This section builds upon the work done by Victor Reyes and George Chen during their time at MIT's Device Realization Lab. Reyes and Chen developed a Digital Twin for Sterlite's optical fiber drawing tower. Through leveraging computational techniques, digital twins are increasingly being explored as a means of improving the performance of physical entities. [28] During the fiber extrusion process, detailed in Section 2.2, data is being recorded and logged by industrial computers into considerably large CSV files. Each file contains one week's worth of data where the process parameters, such as the measured BFD, tension, furnace power, preform speed, capstan speed and others, are recorded and stored. The model created by Reyes and Chen used four inputs to model the diameter of the produced fiber. Those inputs are the preform speed, the capstan speed, helium temperature and the furnace power. However, this research project, in an effort to optimize the model for the draw tower, uses an updated black box to model the drawing tower, shown in Figure 30 below.

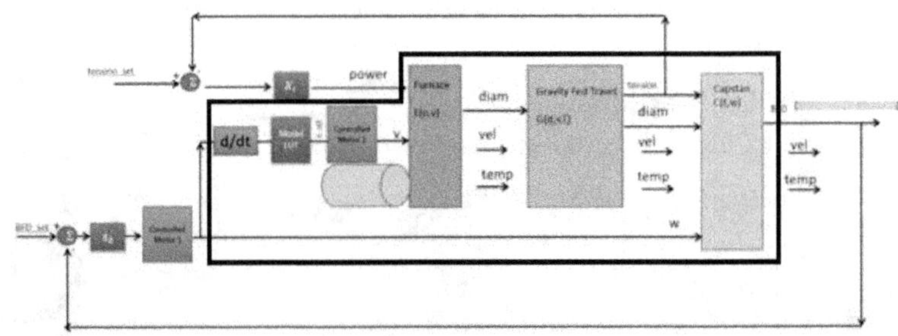

Figure 30: Updated Black Box for Draw Tower Model

The updated black box model takes into it the preform velocity controller. The preform velocity controller involves a discrete look-up table that correlates the slope of the capstan speed to the preform speed. Since the preform velocity controller only involves discrete operations, it was included in the black-box model to optimize the model. As the result, the model trained has 5 inputs compared to the 4 previously mentioned, with the addition of the variable, *rampupslopevalflt,* that corresponds to the slope of the capstan speed, and is training on two outputs, which are the BFD and the tension. Moreover, each week's worth of data was considered as a batch and each contiguous region of production data between 1500 and 8000 data points was considered a sub-batch. Sub-batches were limited to the maximum batch length of 8000 data points in order to normalize the input size to the neural network and to facilitate its training. A snapshot from one week's worth of data is shown below in Figures 31 and 32 for the input and output data, respectively.

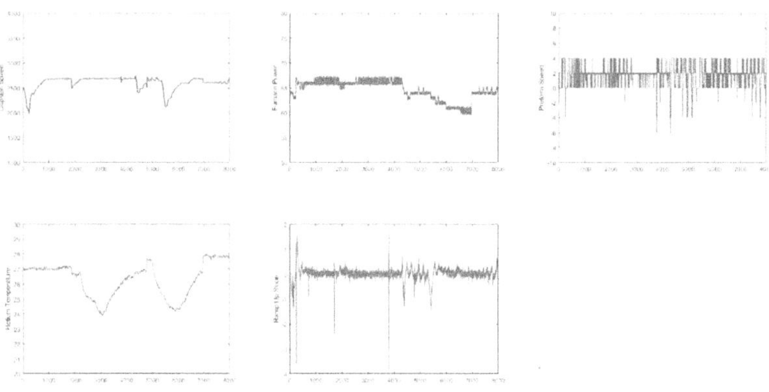

Figure 31: Time-Series Data for the 5 Inputs

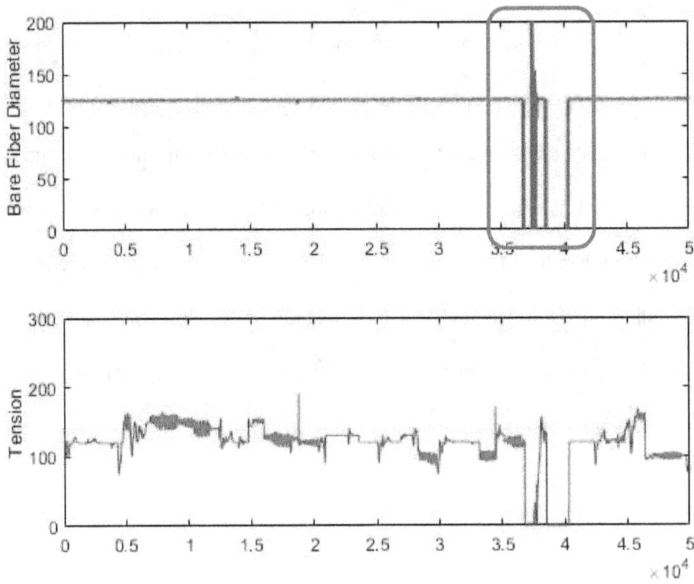

Figure 32: Time-Series Data for the Outputs of the Model

Breaks in the fiber happen throughout the manufacturing process, as highlighted in Figure 32. The breaks could be the result of overheating, coating defects and other irregularities in the coating material. [19] Breaks are also part of the nature of the process because as the fiber is collected on the spools and the spool reaches its required weight, the process has to be stopped for the spool to be replaced with a new one and the extrusion process is resumed. This process is performed manually by operators who would manually stop the process, change the spool, and then bring the tower into operation again. This process results in parts of the data where there is variation as the system is trying to stabilize at the required diameter of 125 microns. In order to remove the transient data as the system is to reach the setpoint of 125 microns, upper and lower limits on the data were placed at 124 and 126 microns, respectively. This would result in the model training better on the BFD output as it doesn't have to account for the transients in the system while training the model.

4.2.1 Re-Sampling and Sub-Batching

Sterlite has two drawing towers that are under investigation in this research project, which are Tower 48 (T48) and Tower 51 (T51). Tower 48 has twelve weeks' worth of data while T51 has five weeks' worth of data. The data received from Sterlite in the form of large CSV files with each CSV representing one week's worth of data was thought to be sampled at 500 milliseconds (ms). All the precious work that was done with Sterlite was based on the assumption that the data was accurately sampled. However, after careful inspection of the data, it was found that the data was randomly sampled which was affecting the accuracy of training of the model. The MATLAB code for processing the data, available in Appendix B, was modified to take into account the random sampling of the data. In order to analyze the effect of resampling the data to be uniformly sampled, the Mean Square Error (MSE) generated by training a model on week of data and testing on all the other weeks was generated for the BFD. Figures 33 and 34 below show the MSE for the training done on T48 and T51, respectively. It is evident from the figures below that the uniform sampling results in better training for the model which results in a lower MSE when the model is tested for other weeks.

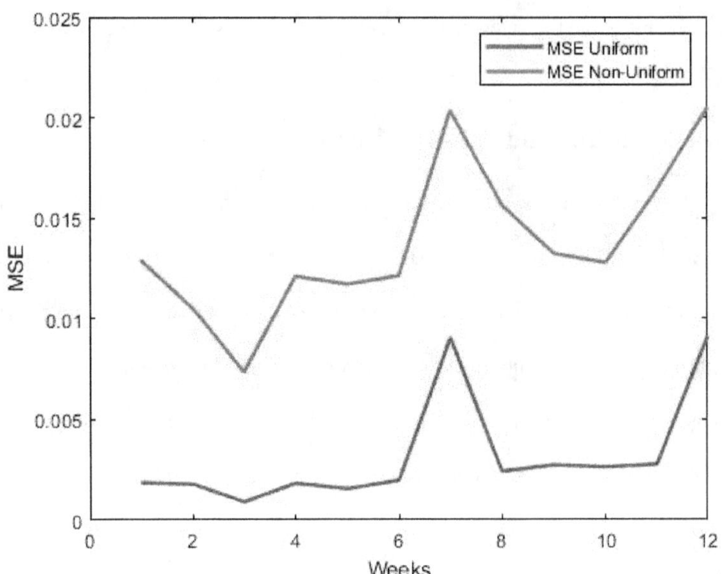

Figure 33: Effect of Re-Sampling Data on MSE for T48

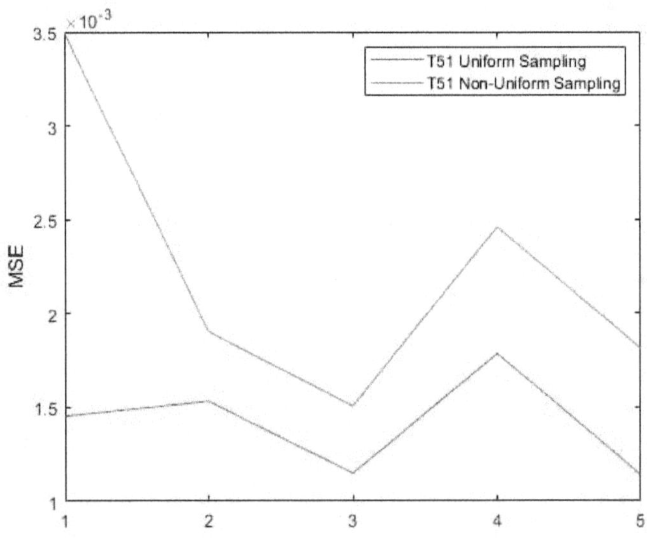

Figure 34: Effect of Re-Sampling Data on MSE for T51

Furthermore, the data was divided into sub-batches for ease of training of the model with each contiguous region of fiber production more than 1500 data points is considered a sub-batch. Sub-batches were limited to maximum sub-batch length of 8000 points to normalize the input to the training model. Initially, as mentioned is Section 4.1, the sub-batching was made on the diameter with upper and lower limits of 124 and 126 microns, respectively. The results of the sub-batching on BFD are shown below in Figure 35.

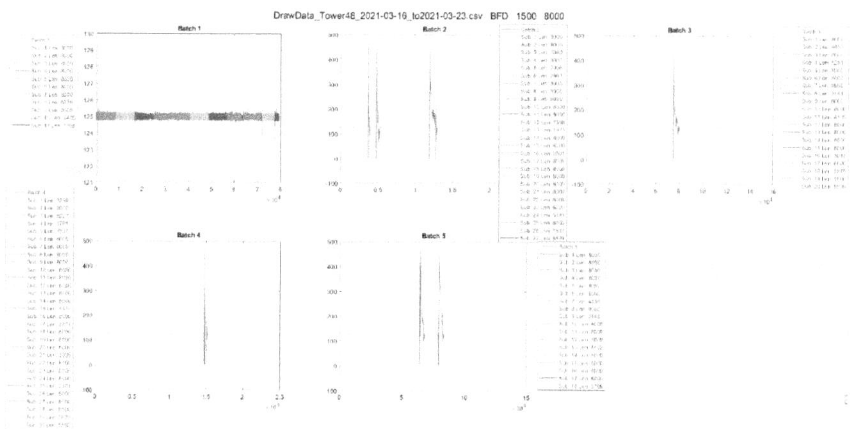

Figure 35: Sub-Batching on BFD

Using the above sub-batching yielded satisfactory results when training the model on the single output of BFD. However, when the same data processing and sub-batching was used to train the model on two outputs, the BFD and the tension, the model wouldn't converge. The results of training the model using 5 inputs on the 2 outputs is shown below in Figure 36.

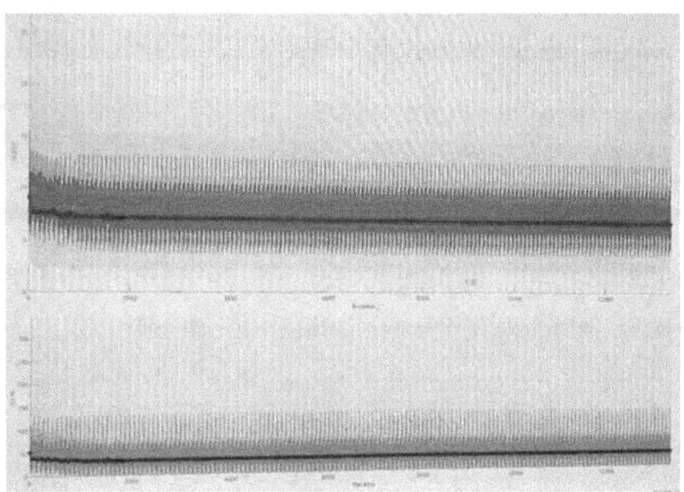

Figure 36: Model Training on Two Outputs using BFD Sub-Batching

The data was explored further to determine the reason behind the non-convergence of the model, and it was found that the tension data is not aligned with the BFD data and that there is considerably more variation and noise in the tension data which is the reason why the model was not converging on the two outputs. Figure 37 below shows the time-series data for both BFD and tension, which highlights the noise in the tension data described above.

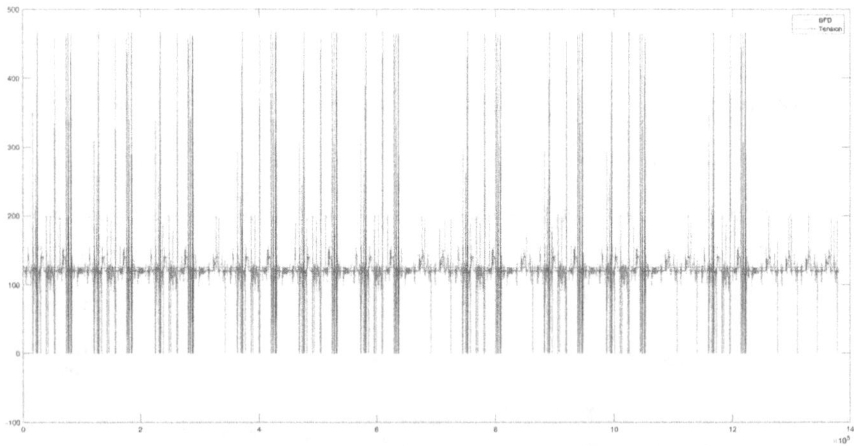

Figure 37: Time-Series Data for BFD & Tension taken from one week's worth of Data for T48

An experiment was performed on the sub-batching to see it's effect on the model, where the sub-batching was made on the BFD and then on the tension to take into account the high noise and variation in the tension data. The tension data normally has values in the range of 120 to 160 N and thus the upper and lower limits used for the tension data are 100 and 200, respectively. The results of the sub-batching based on the tension data is shown below in Figure 38.

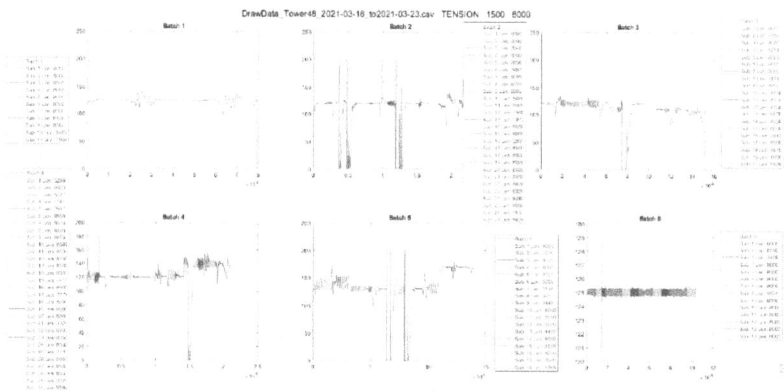

Figure 38: Sub-Batching on Tension Data

The model was then trained using the new sub-batching on two outputs using 5 inputs, and the results are shown below in Figure 39. The model was trained with the hyperparameters listed in Table 3 below.

Hyperparameter	Value
Max Epochs	250
Mini-Batch Size	16
Gradient Threshold	10
Initial Learning Rate	0.005
Learn Rate Drop Period	200

Table 3: Hyperparameters used for Model Training

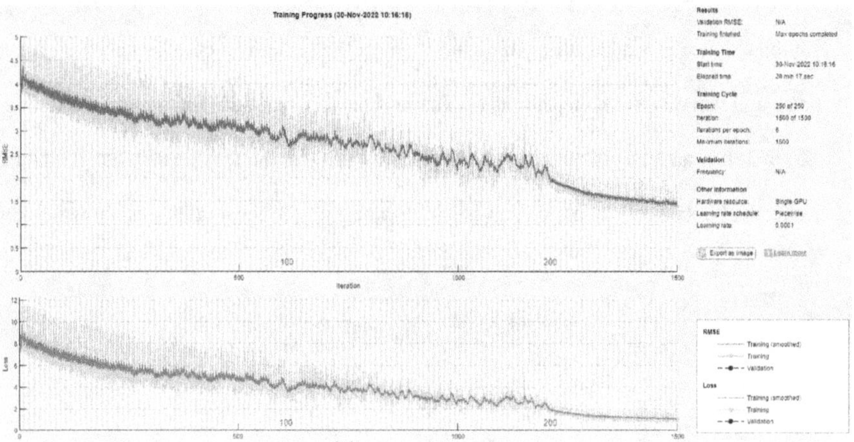

Figure 39: Model Training after New Sub-Batching for Two Outputs Using Five Inputs

The above model was trained with a single LSTM layer of 256 hidden nodes. Experiments were then performed to determine the best neural network architecture to be used to for the surrogate model for the optical fiber draw tower.

4.2.2 Architecture Experiment

After training the model as described in Section 4.2.1, different network architectures were tested to determine the best architecture that achieves the best results while training. Four different architectures were tested to determine the best one using the 5 inputs, mentioned in Section 4.2 to train on the two outputs, which are the BFD and Tension. The four architectures were tested for both T48 and T51 to validate the results of the experiment. The four architectures tested are the simple LSTM, a BiLSTM, a Deep LSTM and a Side-by-Side LSTM networks. The simple LSTM is described in detail in section 3.4 above. The BiLSTM consists of two LSTM layers where one feeds the input to the network in the forward direction and the other feeds it in the backwards direction [29] in order to learn information from preceding as well as following datapoints. [30] The Deep LSTM is a neural network with several LSTM layers stacked one after the other while the Side-By-Side LSTM is stacked horizontally and there is concatenated into a single layer. Figure 40 below gives an illustration of the different LSTM network architectures tested.

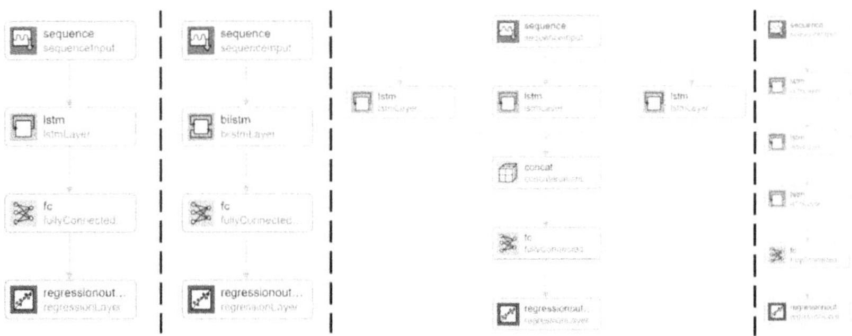

Figure 40: Illustration of LSTM Network Architectures Tested. From Left to Right - Simple LSTM, BiLSTM, Side-By-Side LSTM & Deep LSTM

The results of training using the different network architectures were compared to determine the architectures that achieves the lowest MSE while training. Figure 41 below shows the results of the training using the BiLSTM network architecture on T48.

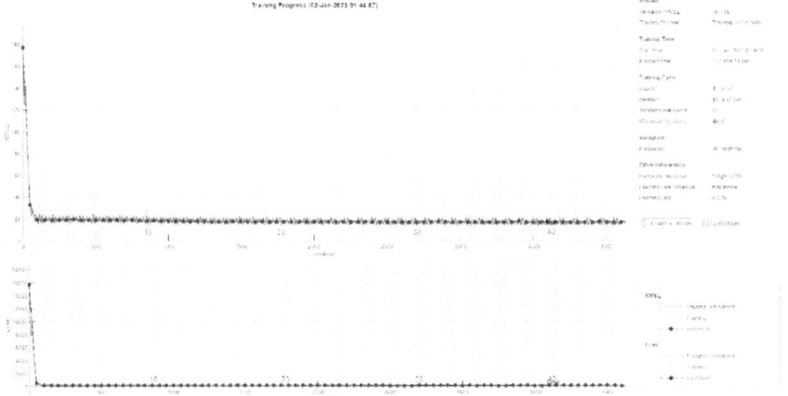

Figure 41: Training Results using BiLSTM Network Architecture for T48

Tables 4 and 5 below provide a summary of the MSE achieved while training the models for T48 and T51, respectively, using the different network architectures.

Network Architecture	MSE
Simple LSTM	17.882
Deep LSTM	19.494
BiLSTM	16.738
Side-By-Side LSTM	18.93

Table 4: MSE Comparison for T48 on the Different Network Architectures

Network Architecture	MSE
Simple LSTM	6.7499
Deep LSTM	6.2485
BiLSTM	5.7401
Side-By-Side LSTM	6.3067

Table 5: MSE Comparison for T51 on the Different Network Architectures

Tables 4 and 5 shows the results of training the neural networks for T48 and T51, respectively, using the different network architectures discussed. It is shown that the BiLSTM network preforms best in terms of MSE for both towers. Table 6 below shows the MSE on the BFD data when training the model on one week of data for T51 and testing on all other weeks for the five weeks of data present for T51.

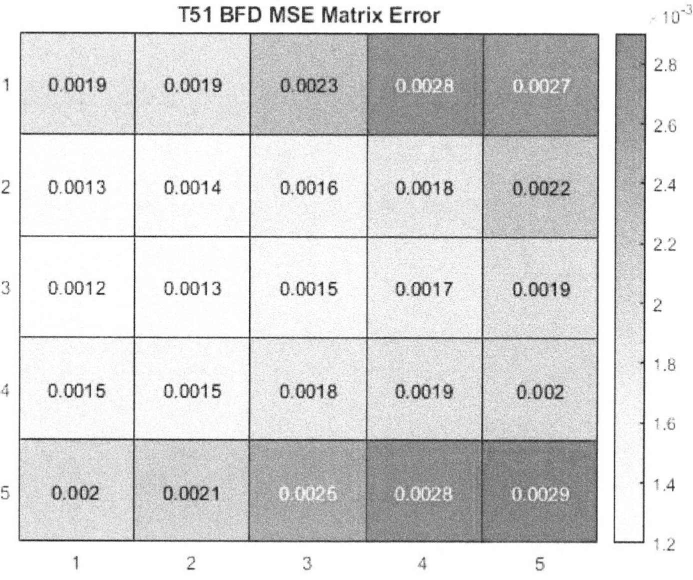

Table 6: T51 BFD MSE Matrix

The results show that the MSE for the BFD is very low, which suggests that the higher MSEs observed in Tables 4 and 5 are due to the error in the tension prediction, which is consistent with the fact the tension data has a lot of noise compared to the BFD data. The output of the LSTM network is then plotted against the actual data to examine the accuracy be of the model in its prediction. The below figures show the output predicted by the different LSTM network architectures compared to the actual data for Tower 51.

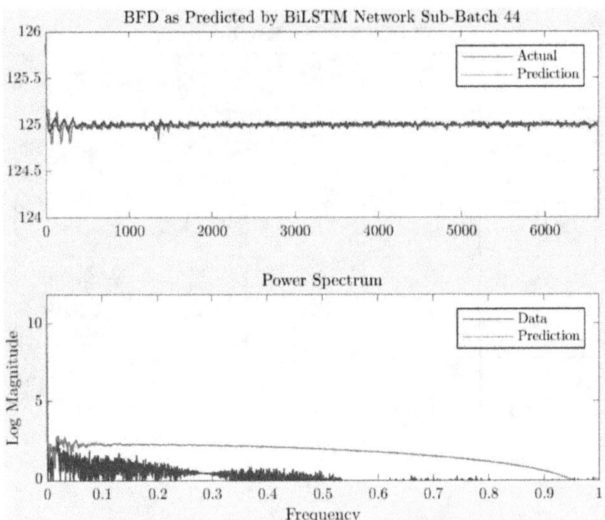

Figure 42: BFD as Predicted by BiLSTM Network for T51

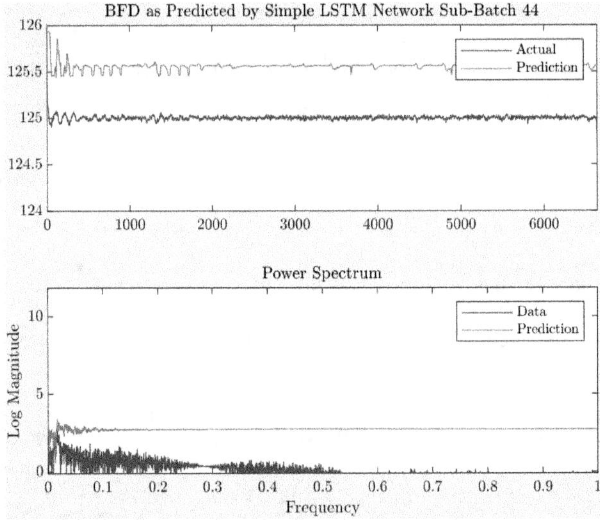

Figure 43: BFD as Predicted by Simple LSTM Network for T51

Figures 42 and 43 above show the BFD results of the model trained on two outputs for T51 using the BiLSTM and Simple LSTM network architectures, respectively. Moreover, the tension predicted by the models trained on the two outputs using the BiLSTM and Simple LSTM network architectures are shown below in Figures 44 and 45, respectively.

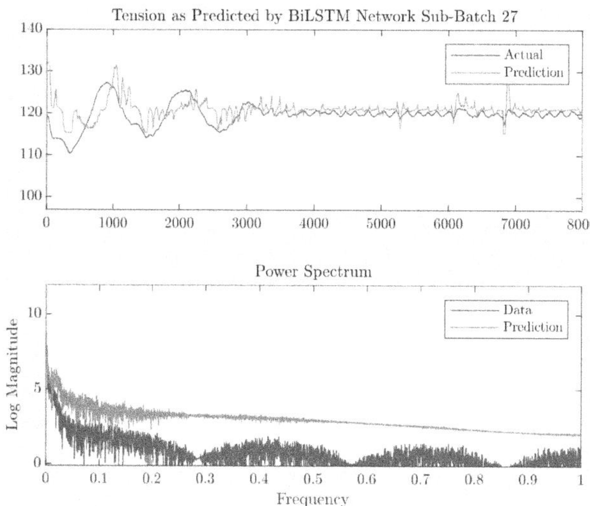

Figure 44: Tension as Predicted by BiLSTM Network for T51

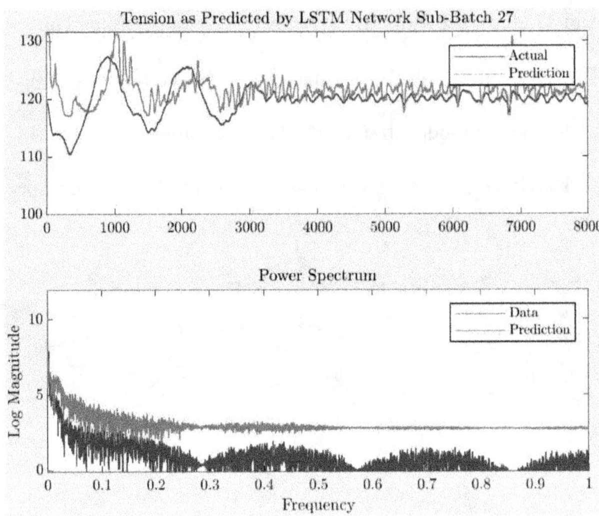

Figure 45: Tension as Predicted by Simple LSTM Network for T51

Chapter 5: Results and Discussion

Chapter 5: Results and Discussion

5.1 Results

The results presented in Section 4.2.2. show that the BiLSTM network preforms best when training on multiple outputs. Previous iterations of this process to create a surrogate model for the optical fiber draw tower resulted in the conclusion of the Deep LSTM being the network that performs best in predicting the output of the model. However, the result of training the same model using a Deep LSTM, shown below in Figure 46, appears to be a straight line that doesn't capture the inherent dynamics of the system, which is also evident from the power spectrum.

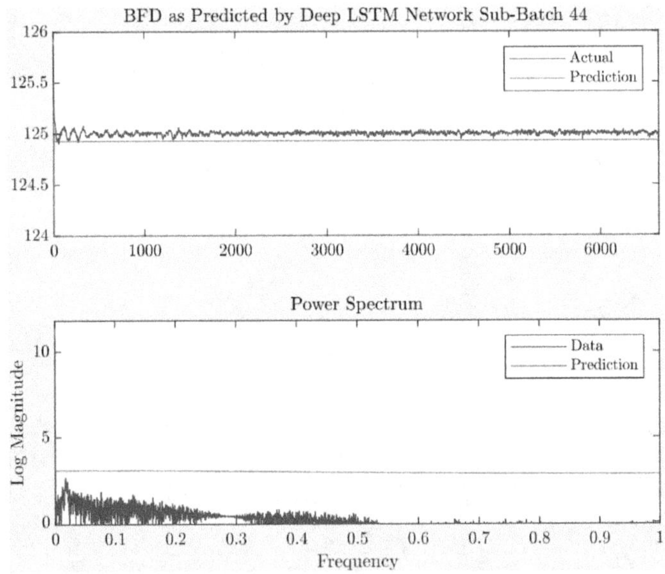

Figure 46: BFD as predicted by Deep LSTM Model

In order to examine whether the above results are due to a bug in the code or due to the coded architecture of the Deep LSTM network, another model was trained using the BFD as the only output and the results predicted by that model compared to the actual data are shown below in Figure 45.

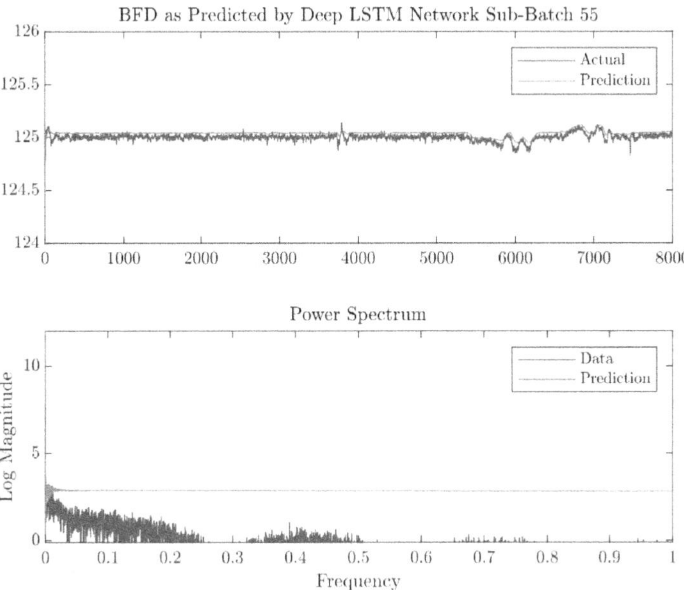

Figure 47: BFD as Predicted by LSTM network Trained on One Output (BFD)

Figure 47 shows that the results of the model trained on only one output with a Deep LSTM follow the actual data closely and perform a good job in predicting the dynamics in the output. This shows that the Deep LSTM is not effective in training on several variables as it doesn't achieve enough learning to capture the dynamics of the system. Moreover, the Side-By-Side LSTM exhibit similar behavior to the Deep LSTM when trained on multiple outputs.

73

Furthermore, the additional sub-batching done by sub-batching on the BFD and then on the tension results in removing most of the dynamics from the data as seen from the actual data from the figures above. An experiment was conducted where the model trained on two outputs was used tested using data that was sub-batched only on BFD to observe how well it learns the dynamics of the system. The result of pre-processing the data by sub-batching only on BFD allows for a lot of dynamics to be included in the data. However, the model that was trained on the two outputs with the additional sub-batching fares better when the data is stable and does not fare as well when there are dynamics in the system as evident from Figure 48 below. This shows the need for iterations on the pre-processing of the data that allows for the model to converge and train well on the sub-batched data while allowing for the dynamics of the system to be modeled. This is highlighted and discussed further in Section 6.2.2.

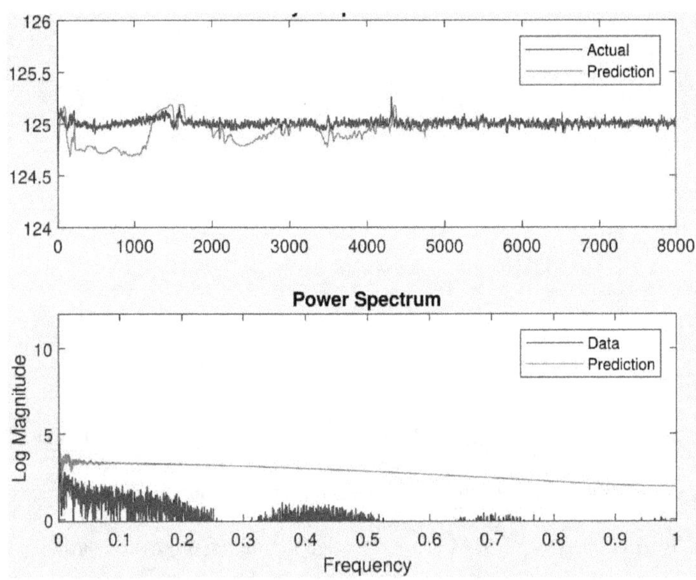

Figure 48: BFD as Predicted by Model Trained on Two Outputs and Tested on Data Sub-Batched Only on BFD

As a result, the BiLSTM appears to be the best network architecture to train on multiple outputs concurrently. This is more time and computationally efficient as it doesn't require to train on the different outputs separately to achieve good prediction results.

5.2 Discussion

The network architectures used in this book are the Simple LSTM, Deep LSTM, BiLSTM and the Side-By-Side LSTM. The details and architecture of those networks are discussed in detail in Section 4.4.2. The BiLSTM network gives the best performance in terms of Root Mean Square Error (RMSE) compared to the other network architectures. However, the applicability of using BiLSTM networks to perform real-time predictions is questioned. This is due to the nature of the BiLSTM network which examines the data in the forward direction and then again in the backwards direction, while the nature of real-time production data follows the natural sequence of time. A lot of research has been and is conducted to test the application and accuracy of BiLSTM networks in time-series forecasting and prediction. YSiami-Namini et al. compared the accuracy of LSTM and BiLSTM networks in predicting stock market performance using historical data and comparing the results of the models to actual stock market performance. [31] They found that the BiLSTM network outperforms the traditional LSTM network by 37.78% reduction in error rates. [31] A lot of research has been conducted to develop different variations of BiLSTM networks to be used in different settings and environments. Hao et al. used a BiLSTM-Attention model to predict atmospheric temperatures. [32] The Attention mechanism is very useful in time series prediction as it allocates computational power to neural networks to "improve the problem of unfocused and time-consuming feature extraction." [32] Moreover, BiLSTM networks have been used to accurately predict short-term traffic flow for urban road sections. [33] BiLSTM networks with Linear Discriminant Analysis (LDA) have also been deployed in industrial settings for fault detection. [33] Muthulakshmi et al. developed a modified neural network model that makes use of the Red Deer Algorithm (RDA) [36] along with a BiLSTM RNN (RDA-BiLSTM) that gave superior results in anomaly detection in cyber-physical systems. [35] Furthermore, a BiLSTM network with a Deep Autoregression Feature Augmentation (DAFA-BiLSTM) have been successfully tested on real-world time series data and it has shown superior adaptive performance and more robustness even with noisy data compared to conventional LSTM and BiLSTM Networks. [37] Last but not least, Zhang et al. developed a Digital Twin Shop floor (DTS) that utilizes a BiLSTM neural network to predict the DTS operation status. Moreover, in an application of BiLSTM neural networks in the Oil & Gas industry, Al-Radhi et al. incorporated a BiLSTM network connected into the control loop of a PLC to control degassing stations in real-time. The block diagram that shows the connection of the PLC to the BiLSTM network is shown in Figure 49 below.

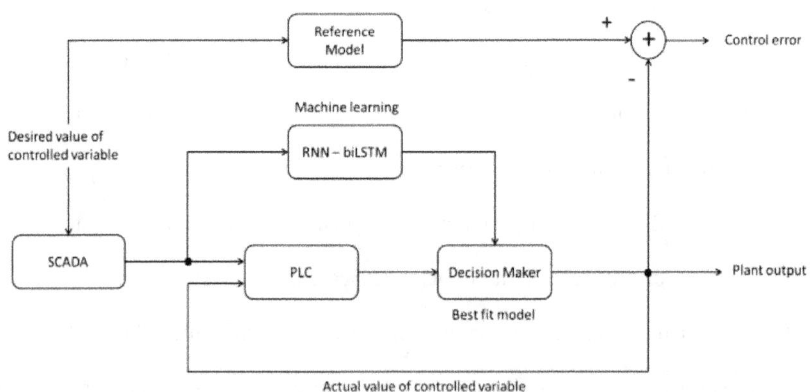

Figure 49: Block Diagram for Integration of BiLSTM network with PLC [39]

The ample research and literature available that shows the superior performance of BiLSTM neural networks in time-series forecasting lends itself to the applicability of using BiLSTM networks in real-time prediction of time-series of data. Moreover, the application of BiLSTM networks with PLCs in the Oil & Gas industry is transferable to a manufacturing setting and could be applied to the control of Sterlite's optical fiber drawing tower in real-time. Moreover, Sterlite proposed the CompactLogix 5480 PLC to be deployed on their production floor to be used along with the surrogate model developed for the process. The CompactLogix 5380 industrial PLC used in conjunction with FrED, as a proof-of-concept, is an earlier version of the PLC proposed by Sterlite. The proof-of-concept test on the current setup, when successful with the older PLC version, can be successfully and efficiently transferred to the newer PLC version with minor modifications.

Chapter 6: Conclusion

Chapter 6: Conclusion

6.1 Contribution

The contributions of this research to Sterlite and to the manufacturing community at large are manifold. The process highlighted in this research project is the start of the process of deployment of Machine Learning models on PLCs to be used in industrial process control. The process for using a desktop fiber extrusion mini-tower, FrED, as a proof-of-concept for the deployment of Machine Learning models on industrial PLCs. The connections made to be able to control FrED through the PLC are provided in Section 4.1 above while the way forward and the work that needs to be completed to bring this project to fruition is highlighted in Section 6.2. Moreover, the process to develop a surrogate model for Sterlite's optical fiber drawing tower was detailed and future work to further optimize the model, to reach better prediction accuracy, is highlighted below. Furthermore, this book studies the applicability of using BiLSTM networks in making real-time predictions of time-series data in real-life manufacturing settings. Finally, this book paves the way for the deployment of a ML model onto an industrial PLC, in the optical fiber industry, to control the parameters of the produced fiber in real-time and to make sure that the fiber produced is within the required specifications. The findings from this book and the related future work could be transferrable to different industries and sectors, where it would make process control more reliable and efficient.

6.2 Future Work

The work presented throughout this book is part of a long-term project with Sterlite with the end goal of deploying a ML model onto an industrial PLC to control the production of their optical fiber draw towers. There are several areas of this work that warrant future research and work towards achieving the end goal of this multi-phase project.

6.2.1 Future Work on PLC

As discussed in Section 4.1, the fiber extrusion mini-tower (FrED) was connected and controlled by an industrial PLC similar to what is planned to be deployed on the shop floor at Sterlite's facilities. The next step in the process would be to develop a feedback loop to control the diameter of the fiber produced by FrED to be within the required specifications. The surrogate model developed for the process is to be used along with previous work developed by Chen [19] to model the controllers of the process to determine the optimized gains of the PLC to maintain the fiber at the required setpoint. This is to be tested on FrED along with the current PLC as a proof-of-concept of the process. Given the success of this process, this would be replicated using Sterlite's real-time production data to determine the optimized one-time gains for their existing controllers on the physical shop floor. This would bring Phase 1 of this multi-phase project to completion. The second phase of the project would be to continuously update the gains of the controllers as the diameter of the fiber drifts out of control to bring in it back to the required setpoint. The third phase would be to utilize new hardware, namely the CompactLogix 5480, proposed by Sterlite, along with the developed ML model to automate the gain settings change process through the PLC's PID control loop. The fourth and final phase of the project is to go beyond the traditional PID control systems and utilize new hardware and new algorithms for the entire process to be completely automated without the need for human intervention.

6.2.2 Future Work on ML Model

Various methods could be used to optimize the ML model developed to lower the RMSE and to make sure that the model's prediction follows closely the actual data and that the inherent dynamics of the process are modeled correctly by the ML model. Firstly, the sub-batching performed to sub-batch the diameter on both the BFD and tension could be optimized in terms of the range of data taken into consideration. The current thresholds are 100 and 200 N.m. for the tension as the actual tension values fluctuate greatly. Several iterations could be run using different thresholds to determine the best threshold values for the sub-batching which allows for taking the dynamics of the system into account while at the same time allowing for the model to converge while training using two outputs. After performing these iterations and the successful pre-processing of the data, several experiments could be conducted to determine the robustness and generalizability of the trained model. These experiments include, but are not limited to, using the model trained on T48 and testing on T51 and vice versa. Another experiment would be running an optimization on the filter length of the filter applied to the raw data to determine the response trained model to the filtering of the data in terms of the RMSE. Finally, the closed loop simulation, utilizing the code developed by Chen [19], is to be conducted to have an simulated model for the entire process with its controllers. Moreover, the current model is trained on data sampled at 500 ms intervals, while the real production data is sampled at 100 ms. The models are to be retrained on the 100 ms data and the experiments to be conducted on the new data in order to have a more accurate surrogate model for the Sterlite's optical fiber draw tower. A recommendation would be to investigate the Sterlite's tension sensor to determine the reason for this excessive noise in the data and replace it with another sensor which would aid in the training of the model and would result in capturing the dynamics of the system better without the interference of excessive noise.

6.3 Conclusion

This book presented the first steps towards the deployment a ML model onto an industrial PLC in the optical fiber manufacturing industry to control the diameter of the produced fiber. Firstly, this book made use of a desktop version of a fiber extrusion tower to connect it to a PLC as a proof-of-concept for using a ML model to control Sterlite's physical production tower. The different phases of the project to reach the end goal of fully and automatically controlling the diameter of the produced optical fiber using ML models are highlighted. Moreover, a surrogate model for the optical fiber extrusion process using RNN networks to model the process was developed. Different LSTM network architectures were examined to determine the best architecture to model the process. Finally, recommendations for future research were given for this project to reach its final stage.

www.ingramcontent.com/pod-product-compliance
Lightning Source LLC
Chambersburg PA
CBHW050606160726
48003CB00003B/1072